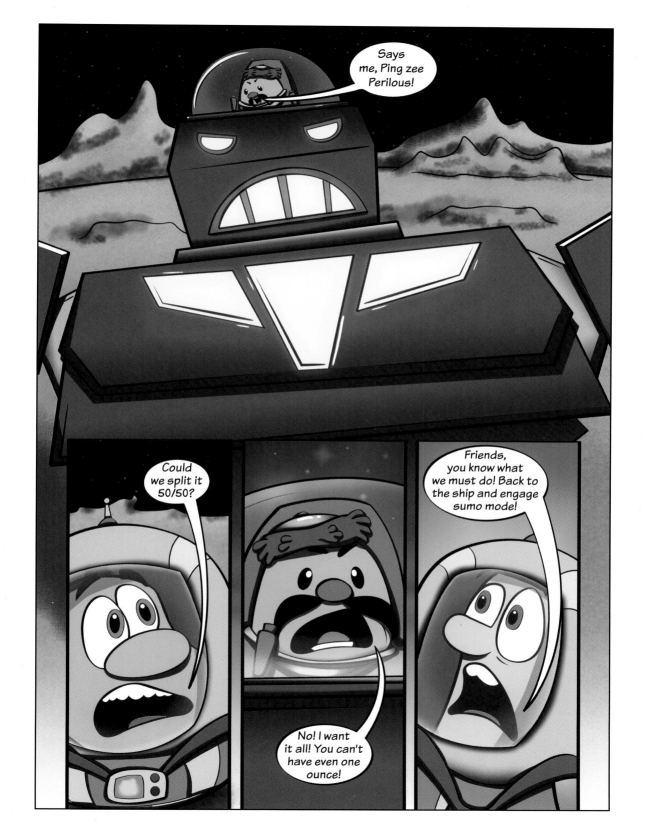

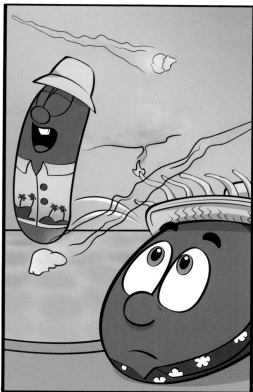

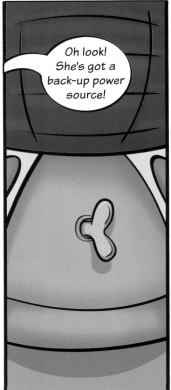

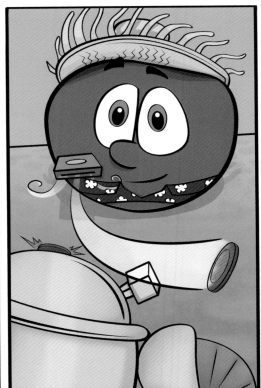

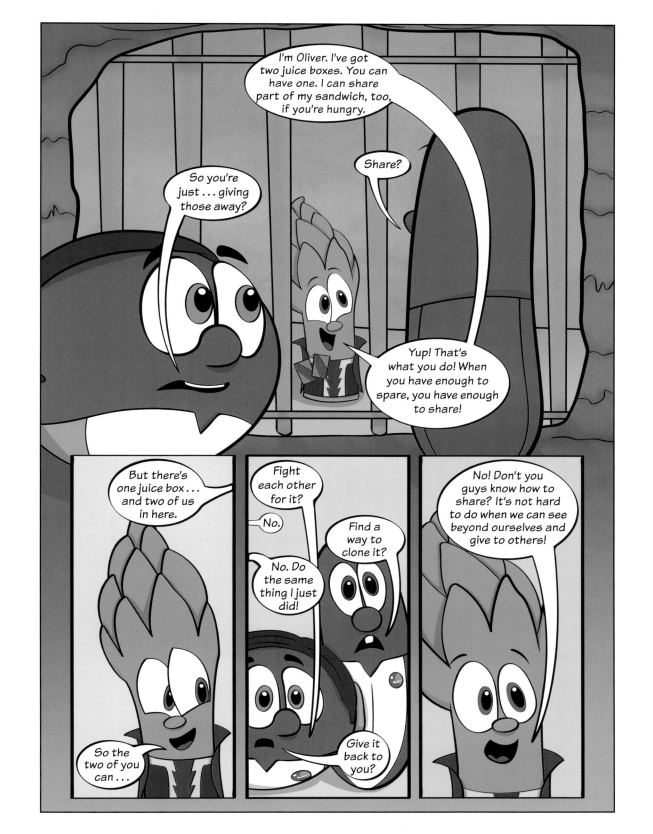

This concept of sharing is . . . logical.

Wait a minute. Are you trying to butter us up to get information for Luntar the Locker Upper?

That's not his name! We call him Luntar the Brave. He's fighting for the whole planet! Tootanny's sun is dying. If we don't find a solution, it will explode into a supernova and destroy the whole planet!

A supernova? That explains why he's been stealing power. He wants to recharge the sun!

Back on the planet . . .

Luntar, the prisoners have escaped!

What?!? Ready my ship and power up the Grabber!

"He who has two tunics, let him give to him who has none; and he who has food, let him do likewise."—Luke 3:11 NKJV